Stars, Fire, I Miss You

Dimitri Blake

BookLeaf
Publishing

India | USA | UK

Presentation by *BookLeaf Publishing*

Web: www.bookleafpub.com

E-mail: info@bookleafpub.com

ISBN: 9789358738223

First edition 2023

Memory

And when I am gone
How will they remember me
Will they say he was a warrior
Fighting injustice at every turn
With bloodied knuckles and gritted teeth

Will they remember my words
And the feelings they inspired
Sadness and glory in equal parts
Soothing whispers and ragged shouts

Maybe they will speak of my accomplishments
He could fence you know
And his food, divine

But most of all
I hope they say
He was kind

Flowers

When people ask how I feel about my friends
I tell them that they're lovely
Excitable
Motivated
They're good people I say

I never mention the fear that lies deep in my
bones
Filling my arteries and lungs
Such a close part of me
That to consider life without it seems foul and
wrong

I don't fear them discovering some horrible sin
Or deciding I'm not worth their time, or their
effort
I don't fear them leaving

I fear that when they leave
I'll think they were right

Worship

It's a weekly ritual of sorts
Gathered here in the kitchen
Elbows bumping and voices raised
We worship together
In this holiest of places
Hands turning over onions and carrots
Pots bubbling over hot flames
We can talk here
With no judgement or fear
It's always easier when your hands are busy
And when there is nothing left to be done
When the benches are wiped
And the stoves extinguished
The silence is just as warm

Beatrijs

You always love my stories
And I love to tell them
But somehow you never realised they're all
shadows of each other
Changing people and places to retell it over and
over
Your own personal theatre
But really, it's all the same
It's a story of how I loved you
And it's a story of how I left

Reflections

The moon spoke to me today
Her voice drifting down
In beams of light
And reflections in shop windows

She told me about you
How you sometimes sit
And stare at her for hours
Or lie with your head in your hands

She told me not to worry though
About the times when I can't be there
When the breath sticks in your chest
And the fear steals away your strength

She told me she would look after you
Silent and warm
Keeping you company
In beams of light
And reflections in shop windows

Zofia

Recently, as I drove home from a day well spent
I pulled over on the side of the highway
My hands stiff and legs growing numb
It was only then I noticed my companions in this
short break
A field of sunflowers, standing tall and proud

Did you know they turn to face the sun, no
matter where they grow?
How amazing
How wonderful
Even plants know to turn their faces to that
which gives them life
Following it across the sky
To soak up warmth and light

And if you did know
Then I have to wonder
Why are you surprised
That I follow you so?

Driving

At home
The lights are on
The house is full of love and dishes and fear
The books stack precariously
And the glow of my laptop shines over fabric
and notebooks
My stresses and disappointments live here with
me
Obvious in chores left undone and unhealthy
choices
But right now there is the road, the radio and us
And I've never been happier

Lilavati

I hope you live a small life
With no great duties or battles
Full of warmth and light
I hope the sun's rays cradle you and winters cold
finds you well dressed and wrapped in blankets
I hope you have hot drinks and cool evenings
I hope you have tables filled with friends and
laughter
And most of all
I hope that when you are gone
The memory of you is kept alive

Conclusions

I tried to write you a poem
To say how much you meant to me
But the words dragged their feet

Unused to coming at the call of happiness and
light rather then the storm of heartbreak they so
often reply to

It was as I sat, thoughts tumbling
That you called me
A short conversation
Full of accusation and betrayal

And as I hung up
I thought to myself
I guess I should thank you
For giving me an ending

Aesa

You're an open book
With dog eared pages
And oily fingerprints
Parts of your spine broken
To let him into the places he sought
Delicate binding ignored
Caring only for what he could take from you

Remember

Will you remember?

You always asked me this
After every adventure
Every heartbreak
Every page in our story together

Will you remember?

Of course
How could I not
With your eyes full of stars
And lungs full of fury
You had so much to be angry about
But never at me
How could I forget
Soft lips and softer hands
Never raised in rage as you were taught
But so often tightened in protest
In righteous fury at a world so unfair
So full of injustice

Will you remember?

And there were bad times

Storms and thunder
Mistakes and regrets
When we laughed until tears ran down our faces
Because if we were going to cry it may as well
be in joy
When there was so much distance between us,
When the phone sat silent and heavy
Each sound a hope of contact quickly dashed

Will you remember?

And when that call finally came
From your father instead of from you
It didn't seem real
How could it?
And I as we walked down the aisle
This wooden box heavy on my shoulders
I could hear you ask one me time

Will you remember?

Brick

Please

And if I could
I would take you away from here
We'd get in my car and drive through the horizon
searching for gold that we'd never find

And if I could
I would shoulder this burden
Bending my back to give you one day's relief
God, you're so strong, but even Atlas had his
limits

And if I could
I would bleed for you
Turning veins and arteries into quills and ink
Writing down our every moment so we can
share it again and again

But I can't
And so instead I hold you while you cry
Waiting until I get home to shed my own tears
I sit with you and tell stories
Reminiscing on adventures and heartaches

And when we run out of memories, we make
them up
Filling the silence that covers four unsaid words

Please don't leave me

Storm

For tonight
Let's leave the lights on
Let's sit together neath flickering globes
pretending it's lightning
To accompany the thunder of our breaking
hearts
Let's go through the motions
Finding every embrace that felt so natural
Let's take tonight
Because in the morning
The storm will have passed

Mistakes

This doesn't happen often
But I have no words
Melting down my silver tongue
Making coins to buy back your affection
But nothing I can say will change us

So instead let me just say this
From the bottom of my heart
With my every aspect of me
From blood, breath, and bone
I am sorry

I will carry this with me
Every decision I make
Will be made in your shadow

Breath

Breathe in

Breathe in with the memory of every person
who told you you can't
With the spite of a child who never listened
when they were told to be realistic
With the ache of dreams just out of reach
With the pain of broken bones, unpaid loans and
a single bedroom apartment you'll never afford
to move out of

Breathe in with a generation of like minded
people who believed in themselves when
nobody else did
Who stood firm on ground crumbling beneath
them
Who bit off more than they could chew and
chose to choke rather then give in

Breath in

And when that breath is aching in your chest
When it feels like you can do no more

Breathe out

Breathe out with every person who stood before
you
With every person who looked at hardship and
decided they liked challenges
With every child looking at a broken world with
hope

Breathe out

And when times seem too hard
When you're shaking from exhaustion
When each call home feels less like a
conversation and more like a cry for help

Breathe in

Ari

I watched the news today
For the first time in a while
I remember why I stopped
So much fear and anger
It seems the cracks in the world are growing
And I'm scared of falling in
I remember being young
Believing I could fix everything
Not full of hope
But rage perhaps
And now all I know is I can't save myself
30 years of blows have left my head bowed
My breath catching in my chest
Eyes closed tight to preserve
The moment of peace
Earned by standing
And I know I never deserved better
And I know you do
And I know if I can just pick up your pieces
One more time then they fall
Then maybe that'll be enough

Hope

Never forget

When the light is low

When all seems set against you
And the world itself seems to tremble

I am with you in the dark

Teeth

I bite my tongue
To keep from telling you how much I love you
To remind myself why you're gone
To remember it's better this way
Nights spent alone
Nothing but dashed hopes and broken promises
for company
The light hangs dim and silent above the door
I bite my tongue
And hope the blood keeps me from tasting you

Shattered

Some say a cracked vase is more beautiful for the fall
I hope this is true
Lovely as you are, I could not keep you from breaking

Time

The Greeks called the dawn rosy fingered
But in this I would disagree
To me she is a thief, caught red handed
Stealing away what little time we have left
A bully with scarlet fists, promising new
beatings each day
A bloody challenge to be confronted, gasping
through gritted teeth
I am not done
I am not finished
You cannot have me
And with every crimson sunrise
Rising over the horizon

I am still here

The End

I know how the lonely page must feel, desperate
to stop you turning a new leaf
Because to me

You were the whole book